Uley, Dursley and Cam

IN OLD PHOTOGRAPHS

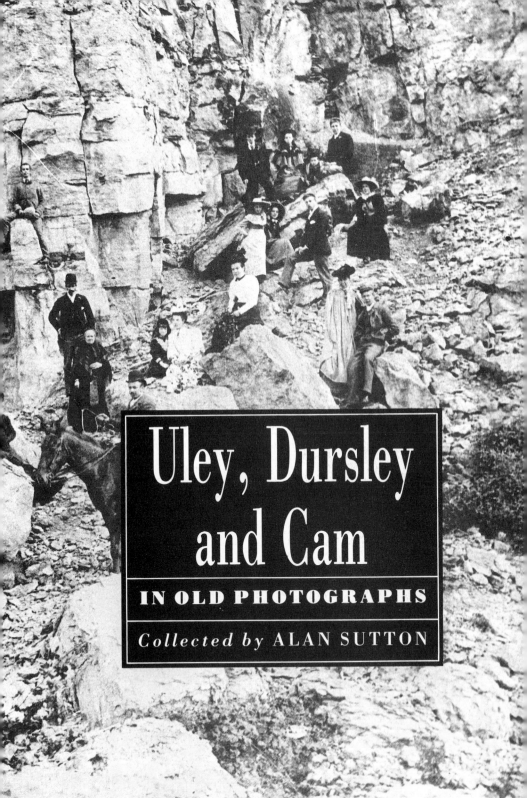

Uley, Dursley and Cam

IN OLD PHOTOGRAPHS

Collected by ALAN SUTTON

Alan Sutton Publishing Limited
Phoenix Mill · Far Thrupp
Stroud · Gloucestershire

First published 1991

Published in Collaboration with the
Cam & Dursley Camera Club.

The detail below is enlarged from the
photograph on page 35. The previous two pages
show the same family, on the same day, posed
for their artistic photograph at Lampern Hill
quarry, some time *c.* 1885.

**British Library Cataloguing
in Publication Data**

Uley, Dursley and Cam in old photographs.
I. Sutton, Alan, *1949–*
942.41

ISBN 0-86299-888-3

Typeset in 8/9½ Sabon.
Typesetting and origination by
Alan Sutton Publishing Limited.
Printed in Great Britain by
The Bath Press, Avon.

Introduction

This selection of old photographs is the third to feature Dursley. In 1981 there was David Evans' pioneering *Dursley and Cam*, and in 1986 he produced a further selection, *Around Dursley in Old Photographs*, this time collaborating with Ann Wilson. Now, after yet another five years, we have *Uley, Dursley and Cam in Old Photographs*. There may have been a change of author, but it still contains many of David's collection of photographs, and a great deal of his help.

Many of the other photographs in this volume come from the extensive collection held by the Cam and Dursley Camera Club, and their help and co-operation is very gratefully acknowledged. Special mention should be made of Bill Turner, the Society archivist, whose photographs of Dursley and Cam in the 1950s and '60s provide a valuable comparison of 'before' with 'after' at the demolition sites in Long Street, the Market Place and at the bottom of Cam Pitch.

The 1986 book concentrated on people; I have purposely taken a different approach, that of a lengthy, circular peregrination which takes the reader on a tour starting and ending at the top of Crawley Hill. Apart from the detours to Owlpen, Cam Peak and the Yew Tree, the walk is approximately thirteen and a half miles, a pleasant summer day's outing, allowing a break for lunch and ending at the Crown for supper. The tour is as follows:

From Crawley Hill to the Green at Uley; to Owlpen and back to the Green; down the Street; part of the way up Lampern Hill; to Shadwell and Elcombe, and past Sheephouse Farm to Woodmancote.

From the top of Woodmancote to the bottom of Bull Pitch. Down Water Street, past Goody Mead to Ferney; back to the Priory and the bottom of Drake Lane; up Long Street to the Market Place; along the Knapp to Rednock, and up Rednock Drive to Kingshill Road. Back towards Dursley and down Parsonage Street and Silver Street. From Silver Street up Boulton Lane, with a detour to the Slade, and on up Union Street to Hunger Hill; down the hill the other side, into May Lane, and up Hill Road to Broadway. Then a trip through the beech woods, at first keeping to the path at the bottom of Westfield Wood, and then taking Westfield Lane to survey Dursley from Stinchcombe Hill above Sheep Path Wood. Back down the lane, taking the turn to Kingshill. Right at the cinema and down Gasworks Pitch to Upper Cam.

From Littlecombe to Spring Hill and Cam Peak; back to Upper Cam and Hopton Road; past the station to Rowley and on to Chapel Street. A detour to the junction at the Yew Tree and back to High Street; past the Jubilee Tree to Draycott, and on to Coaley Junction, a sad symbol of Dr Beeching's axe. On to Coaley, past Far Green and on to Knapp Lane; through Coaley Wood and back to the top of Crawley Hill.

A great wealth of photographic material comes from the period 1895 to 1920, the heyday of the picture postcard when, before the widespread use of the telephone, everyday communications were short notes sent by post. Capitalizing on this wealth of images, the tour shows the reader how Uley, Dursley and Cam (not forgetting Coaley) looked at the turn of the century. In addition, some of the captions contain lengthy discursions, especially on the woollen industry, the pre-eminent source of employment for the town and surrounding villages.

Why Dursley and its environs are as they look today can be explained by a brief outline of the rise and fall of the woollen trade. Why many of the captions in this book hark back to the 1830s can be accounted for by the same simple explanation – the almost total collapse of the local economy between 1830 and 1837. The following is almost dangerously over-simplified as the subject is complex and deserves a lengthy book all of its own but, in essence, the trade became increasingly important in the sixteenth century, and by the 1580s Dursley had achieved fame, not for the quality of its woollen cloth but for the tricksters who sold sub-standard material wrapped up in better cloth. In Shakespeare's time, the saying 'he is a man of Dursley' was in common usage throughout England to describe sharp practice. Happily, this fell out of use and the town grew in importance as a market and manufacturing town. Mills were powered by the Ewelme rivulet, and this head of water was complemented in Dursley by the springs in Broadwell where it became the Cam, powering at its height some twenty mills from Owlpen through to Cambridge. Finished cloth was taken by pack horse to Blackwell Hall in London, the main cloth mart in England, from where most was exported.

As Dursley grew, it developed into the main agricultural market in the area, being the centre for the trade in Double Gloucester cheeses from the rich pasture lands of the Vale of Berkeley. As a surviving emblem of this high point we have the proud market hall of 1738.

Most employment came from woollen cloth and its associated trades. Dursley specialized in cards made from leather, wood or thick card (hence the name cardboard?) into which wires were drawn and cut to produce an effect similar to a wire brush. These were used extensively in the trade for carding the wool fibres of the thread. In Dursley there were several wire drawers manufacturing the wire, and card makers. It was this trade that brought George Lister from Yorkshire to Dursley in about 1817. He soon became the largest manufacturer and, with Edwin Budding, the inventor of the lawn-mower, developed machinery for the woollen industry on the site of Mawdesley's old factory, Rivers Mill in Uley Road.

In addition to wire drawers and card makers there were mill workers carrying out the following processes: (1) Preparing the wool – sorting, scouring, dyeing, twillying, beating and picking, scribbling, carding. (2) Spinning and preparing the yarn – spinning abb (slubbing), spinning warp (warping), reeling abb. (3) Weaving – sizing, weaving. (4) Producing the cloth – scouring, drying, burling, picking, felting, roughing, cutting, mozing, cutting (again), roller boiling, dyeing, cutting (yet again), picking, marking, brushing, pressing. Production was not a simple process and many men, women and children were employed. The largest, most important and most independent of all the workers were the handloom broadweavers. The weavers worked at home and had cottages with large handlooms taking up much space. Many local cottagees were built with large windows to allow sufficient light for the weaver to see his work, and good examples of these can be seen in Holywell, Woodmancote and in Rowley, Cam.

The main industry around Stroud specialized in the Stroudwater reds. Uley and Dursley specialized in 'blues', and by the 1830s the main cloth manufactured was kerseymere or cassimere, a twilled, fine woollen cloth.

A depression in 1825–6 was severe enough to create weavers' riots and a Uley magistrate called in the military, although this was nothing particularly unusual as highs and lows had been seen in the trade many times before. But it was a portent of what was to come, with a devastating blow, in 1837, when the business of Edward Sheppard, the largest local employer, failed.

The depression of 1837 was the death knell to a great many Gloucestershire clothiers, and the failure of Edward Sheppard in particular was a mortal blow to the Uley valley. Sheppard employed 1,000 people locally, and the significance of this can be judged from a survey of 1838 when the total number employed in the industry in the whole of Gloucestershire was 5,740. In other words, just under one-sixth of the manufacturing capacity of the county was taken out, and this sixth was in our valley.

The problems had been accumulating for many years. As early as 1790, the area was falling behind Yorkshire due to resistance by the workforce to new manufacturing techniques, in particular the automated carding of wool. By 1790 much of the Yorkshire wool was carded by machine but the attempt to introduce such technology in Gloucestershire led to riots. Gloucestershire cloth became more expensive and the market looked to Yorkshire for its supplies, even though the quality of the Gloucestershire cloth may have been higher. By the time of the depression in 1837, clothiers such as Sheppard were trying to catch up by installing steam engines. Sheppard had four huge Boulton and Watt engines in his Uley factory, but in Stroud, with the facility of the Stroudwater Canal, they had the benefit of coal at twelve shillings a ton. In Yorkshire coal was five shillings a ton. In Uley the cost must have been astronomic as coal had to be brought by pack horse or, at best, by horse-drawn wagon. In 1838 the Gloucestershire mills received 34 per cent of their power from steam; in the same year Yorkshire mills were achieving 78 per cent. The end for Gloucestershire was inevitable. Some clothiers did survive and, even to this day, one and a half centuries after the collapse of the main players, Cam Mills is still producing the quality Gloucestershire broad cloth. But the survivors were few and they had to see through the bad times. The way to survival was reduced wages, hasty introduction of technology and general hardship all round.

Uley and Cam were particularly badly hit. Coaley had been depressed to begin with and just continued at this below-subsistence level. Dursley did not escape, but at least offered alternative employment in card manufacturing (albeit at reduced levels) and brewing, producing the cheap anaesthetic that kept people's minds off their humiliating poverty. Beer is extremely nourishing and provides sufficient food value to exist at a base level. It is no exaggeration to say that men, women and children drank to excess, with additional sustenance from poor quality vegetables and the occasional bacon fat. This alcohol-blasted state horrified the Victorian middle class and eventually led to the temperance movement of the mid to late nineteenth century. But life in a squalid one-up, one-down hovel, with filth and disease and crying hungry infants, could not be accepted with equanimity, and the hopelessness of finding no work humiliated weavers and mill workers. In the circumstance drunkenness is not a surprising outcome.

The population of Uley shrank by more than half as many hundreds emigrated to America and Australia. The cottages that sprang up in the first two decades of the century wanted for tenants, and the whole valley settled down to weather through the rest of Queen Victoria's reign. In general, no building took place. The town and adjacent villages quietly stagnated.

Then the phoenix arose with the Lister family. The founder of the Dursley dynasty of Listers was George, who had developed his business from cards to card-making machinery between 1817 and 1860.

Carding engines manufactured by George Lister at River's Mill, *c.* 1860.

By 1860 George Lister was probably the largest employer in Dursley, and his factory was in Uley Road. His third son was Robert Ashton Lister, who became estranged from his father by 1867 and left the family firm to set up his own agricultural machinery business. The last three decades of the century saw two Lister companies in Dursley, the business of the youngest son outstripping the business set up by the father. In 1903, on the death of his eldest brother, William, Robert Ashton bought out his late father's business, which had by then begun producing electric motors and dynamos through the enterprise of Ashton's nephew, James Fraser Lister. By this time the largest part of his late father's business was the Lister Electric Light and Power Manufacturing Company. This company was eventually sold by R.A. Lister to Henry Mawdesley in 1907.

These two businesses have been the mainstay of Dursley and its satellite villages for over a hundred years. Now times are changing, and mobility has removed much of the need for doorstep industries, but it is upon this manufacturing base that the town has developed, and its modern appearance can be directly traced back to the influence of the clothing trade. Dursley is a working town, and has been for centuries. Painswick, Minchinhampton and Tetbury stagnated and, from an employment point of view, died. Because of this they have retained much of their sixteenth-, seventeenth- and eighteenth-century beauty. Dursley did not exactly thrive but, due to entrepreneurial individuals, survived and provided employment for miles around. Now we have to live with the consequences. The success of the town has been its downfall, resulting in the loss of beauty on utilitarian grounds, and this has removed Dursley from the itinerary of Cotswold tourists. Walkers on the Cotswold Way may anticipate an attractive Cotswold town, but lack of suitable hostelries and other appurtenances of a tourist environment force them to press on to other parishes.

Dursley has amazing natural wealth in its surroundings. The valley is one of the most attractive in Gloucestershire; ancient beech woods hang on the hills and create an aspect second to none. But the town – oh dear! Poor post-war planning, abysmal architecture, unsympathetic materials and a noticeable lack of creativity. Would you invest in the opening of a decent new restaurant in such a town?

What we need is the acorn of interest that will grow into the oak tree of achievement. We need developers, but before that we need a civic society that can ensure the development is right and done with taste and sympathy to the needs of a Cotswold town; that looks ahead into the future, and not with the developer's eye for short term profit. We need a supermarket; we need people to shop in the town or it will die. We need to take a hard look at our balance sheet and see what assets we have.

For example, let me point to an unexploited area of our parish that could be a jewel in a revitalized Cotswold market town. Given the will of the property owners, the introduction of intelligent developers, the unblinkered interest of planners and, above all, the guidance of a new civic society, we could make Water Street the centre of the

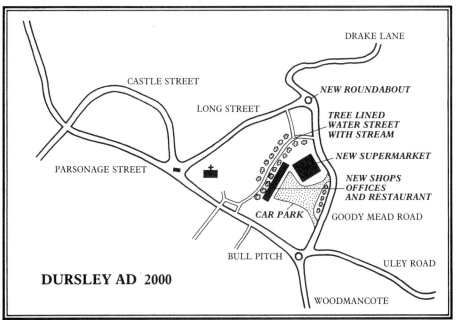

town. There would be a link road from the new roundabout at Woodmancote down Goody Mead to meet the bottom of Long Street, a new supermarket with a large car park as the heart of the development, a pedestrian precinct up Water Street, pleached hornbeams along the paths by the side of the stream, offices in a refurbished Howard's Upper Mill, *bijou* shops – a restaurant even! – perhaps a tourist centre so those poor walkers need not hurry past and, to cap it all, a decent pub and a hotel.

It was not the woollen trade that made Dursley a town. The town was already here and the trade developed within it, taking advantage of the water power provided by the springs and the Ewelme. It could be argued that in a book of old photographs the following paragraphs have little place, but without the castle and without tufa Dursley might never have developed beyond a village and, as such, would not have had sufficient photographs to take an interest in. Every town is where it is for a reason. Dursley exists because of the plentiful fresh water, the importance of the castle as a focal point for local lordly power, and the stone – the tufa – prized by builders of centuries past.

The town name comes from the Saxon for Deorsige's clearing. By the time of Domesday in 1086 it was Dersilege. It was the ancestral home of the Saxon Berkeleys, who had their power base at a castle in Dursley before the Norman conquest of 1066. Roger de Berkeley, Lord of Dursley, was a cousin of Edward the Confessor. This Saxon family were spared the Norman confiscations, and it was only by siding with Stephen in the civil war against Matilda that the estates were lost. In 1154, with the accession of Henry II, the estates were granted to a Norman, Robert Fitz Harding, whose family later took the name of Berkeley. King Henry arranged for marriages between the Fitz Hardings and Berkeleys, with a son of each family marrying a daughter of the other. The king furthermore arranged for the 'Saxon' Berkeleys to have their Dursley estates restored to them, the 'Fitz Harding' Berkeleys building a new castle on their large estates in the vale. Coaley and Cam remained with the 'Fitz Harding' Berkeleys, and were still part of the Berkeley estate up to the mid-nineteenth century.

The Dursley Berkeleys continued in succession until 1382, when the last son of the line died without children. The estate then passed to the Cantelupe family, and later to the Wykes, who dismantled the castle for its stone – the tufa – around 1530 to build their main estate at Dodington. The castle – for it truly did exist – must have stood on the site now covered by the Tabernacle, the minister's house and the corner of the recreation ground behind. It was probably a twelfth-century building replacing a Saxon timber building, and is likely to have been more of a large, fortified manor house than the full scale castle we might envisage.

Writing in the 1540s, Leland said, 'Dursley had a castell in it sum tyme longynge to the Berkeleys, sins to the Wickys, sins fell to decay and it is clene taken down. It had a metelie good ditch about yt, and was, for the moste parte, made of towfe stone, full of pores and holes, lyke a pumice. There is a quarry of this stone about Dursley, and it will last very long.' John Smyth, writing eighty years later, added . . . 'the ruins of which are now fruitfull with barley and wode there growynge.' Samuel Rudder, in his *New History of Gloucestershire* in 1779, recorded that the ruins of its foundations were still visible in a garden adjoining the castle fields.

In 1913, when foundations for the Tabernacle primary school were being built, workmen laid bare very solid masonry that appeared to be the remains of some old vault or cell, round-headed, or Norman, in style. The masonry was so solid that it was incorporated into the present foundations. It seems pretty conclusive that the Tabernacle was the site, and the road sweeping down into the town must originally have been part of the 'metelie good ditch'. The detail of the painting of 1810 reproduced here seems to show a crenellated gateway in the corner of the field, with a child's swing in front. Was this part of a gateway of the ruin?

A detail from the painting below, showing a child's swing and a crenellated gateway.

A painting of the Tabernacle, c. 1810, showing Parsonage Street and the open Castle Farm fields prior to the building phase of 1815.

From the lord's power base to tufa. The quarry would seem to have extended from the back of the bottom of Long Street right through to the stream, possibly even where the Lister-Petter head office stands. The quarry must have been very extensive as we know that much of Berkeley Castle and Dursley Church, not to mention Dursley Castle, are or were built of it. Tufa is also present, of course, in countless other Dursley buildings. The site of the quarry is reasonably confirmed in nineteenth-century histories, although their description of the location is not exactly precise. The site of Rock Cottages and of Rock House is something of a giveaway.

Tufa is, to be precise, calcareous tufa, a porous or vesicular carbonate of lime, generally formed from calcareous springs. It is produced by a build up over millions of years of carbonate of lime deposits from the limestone springs in the Broadwell. This form of tufa is rare and found in only three places in Europe. For building purpose it was admirable. When quarried it was soft and could be cut very easily and yet when exposed to air it hardened to a great strength.

It is still possible to see the remains of Dursley Castle, an example of tufa's versatility, although one has to go to Dodington to do so. The castle lasted for about four hundred years in Dursley, and when dismantled in 1530 the stone was carted the twenty or so miles to Dodington, where the first Dodington House was built of it. This house was in turn demolished in the eighteenth century, but the tufa was used for a third time, and can still be seen today in the eighteenth-century bridges on the Dodington estate.

In such a short space it is not possible to do much more than touch upon the history and development of the town and local industry. An ancient industry developed in Dursley, and then moved back up the stream to Uley and on down the stream to Cam. Water provided the power, and the mills formed in a linear manner to take advantage of it. The mills required workers and the town and villages grew as folk moved in seeking employment. This industrial and social heritage gave rise to the photographs in this book, and I hope that interest in and enjoyment of the Ewelme and Cam valley histories may be shared through them.

Compiling the book has been a great pleasure, but without help from many people who supplied photographs and information it would have been a daunting task. In particular I would like to thank the following: Cam and Dursley Camera Club, Peter Barrell, Howard Beard, David Burton, David Evans, Nicholas Mander, Wilf and Betty Merrett, Archie and Dorothy Sutton, Bill Turner and Matt Welsh.

The selection proved most difficult and, rather than having too few photographs as I originally feared, I ended up having far too many and had to be most selective in what I used. The area's photographic heritage is very considerable, and so there may be more to come!

Alan Sutton
Hydefield
Uley

Natural beauty all around us. A photograph of the Quarry, taken from Stinchcombe Hill *c.* 1900. The Yew Tree Inn is in the foreground, and the elm avenue has much younger trees than those shown on page 145. Quarry Gardens and Woodfields now cover most of the right-hand side of this view. The River Severn, the horseshoe bend and the Forest of Dean are in the distance.

Uley

Two views looking down Crawley Hill. The top picture is of *c.* 1915, the bottom picture, *c.* 1930. Note that the close grazing of the side of Uley Bury has stopped long enough to let some small trees take hold.

The previous two pages show the turnpike and crossroads, *c.* 1905.

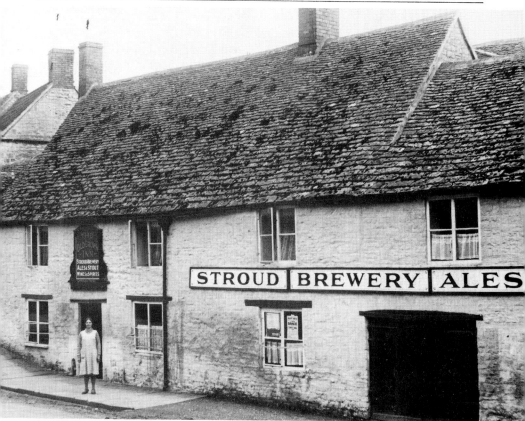

The Old Crown, watering hole to the world, in a photograph of *c.* 1930. In 1776 Boswell records Dr Johnson as saying, 'There is nothing which has yet been contrived by man, by which so much happiness is produced as by a good tavern or inn.' What more can one add, apart from relating an anecdote published in *Gloucestershire Notes and Queries* in 1894 describing an event that occurred many years before. The landlord for much of the first half of the century was John Ferebee. One dark evening a stranger rode up to the door and, after duly refreshing himself, anxiously enquired how far it was to the manor house at Owlpen. 'Surely, Sir, you do not think of going there such a dreary night as this,' replied old Ferebee. 'Indeed I do, for business presses,' answered the traveller, 'but how far, pray, is it, and which way must I turn?' 'Why,' was the answer, 'you must go along the Green and down the hill by Fiery Lane until you come to Cuckoo Brook, then a little further on you will pass Horn Knep, after which you will go by Dragon's Den; next you go through Potlid Green; after that is Marling's End and that will bring you straight into Owlpen, but you must take care not to miss the road.' 'If it be so long and troublesome a way to find, why then landlord, I think, if you have a bed, I will stay till the morning.' So Ferebee gained himself a guest for the night, and the traveller saved himself a long and wearisome journey of not more than ten minutes.

This photograph shows Miss Barbara Paish, daughter of the landlord, Tom Paish. The door and the window behind her have now been changed around so that the entrance to the inn is in the position of the window.

Uley Green and the road to Owlpen. The date is difficult to discern, but possibly between 1915 and 1925.

Owlpen Manor in 1905.

Owlpen Manor, in an amateur photograph of *c*. 1900. The hall of the present manor house was built between 1542 and 1573 by the Daunt family. The west wing, shown here on the left, was added in 1616. Thomas Daunt V made many small additions between 1719 and 1726. After his death in 1749 the house and estate entered a gentle decline. The owners of the estate built a grand mansion, Owlpen Park, on the ridge of the hill to the east in the 1840s, but this was demolished in 1955 and the manor it was built to supplant now thrives, thanks mainly to the efforts of the craftsman Norman Jewson who bought the Manor in 1925. Jewson was a disciple of Ernest Gimson of the Cotswold Arts & Crafts movement, and through his loving care the Manor was brought back to life. It is hard to imagine a more picturesque setting than that enjoyed by Owlpen Manor in this quiet valley.

Two views of Owlpen Manor. The top picture, of *c.* 1900, looks east, towards the hill surmounted by Owlpen Park. The bottom picture is of approximately the same date but a reciprocal view, looking back towards the Manor, with Uley in the distance.

A view of Uley from Owlpen, *c.* 1915, showing the gardens and part of the fields now covered by Green Close. Owlpen was a thriving parish at the end of the eighteenth century. By 1800 the population was over 400; now the population is less than one-quarter of that.

Uley Green and the Old Crown, 1906.

Two views of Uley Feast in 1915. The Green must have been very cramped, but apparently much of the atmosphere of the Feast was due to its being held in such a small space. It is hard to imagine a similar fair being organised here in the 1990s. The proprietors of the fair were called Peters.

A view from the Green, *c.* 1870. The church was rebuilt in 1857–8 to the design of S.S. Teulon. The house next to the church was demolished before 1900. The house this side of the brick house has also now disappeared, but the brick house itself is resplendent with bay windows (see the next page). This fine photograph must have been carefully posed as exposure times in the 1870s were relatively lengthy, and any movement would have meant blurred figures.

Only thirty years before this picture was taken, Uley suffered catastrophe when one of the largest businesses in the area failed. (In 1837 the population of Uley was 2,543. In 1971 it was less than half that, at 1,238. In 1981 there was further decline to 1,154. The figures for 1991 are not yet available.) The woollen cloth business of Edward Sheppard was very extensive and he employed 1,000 local people up to his bankruptcy in 1837. Sheppard's business had grown dramatically in the good times, and he had a grand mansion built at the Ridge, between Dursley and Wotton. At that time he had a gate lodge at Bowcott, and from here it was but a short drive down the valley to his factory. During the weavers' strikes it was Sheppard who led the employers' capitulation and increased wages, and he had a general reputation for fair pay. After his business failure and the collapse of the industry locally Uley stagnated and the population more than halved. Many emigrated to America, Canada and Australia. Those that remained were reduced to great poverty, and William Miles reported in 1839 that, 'The distress, even now, is extreme, and the most suffering are the most silent. Their clothes are daily wearing out, their children are half naked; they have scarcely any bedding, and actually sleep under tattered rags. Every article that would bring money has been sold, and the population is destitute of money, and almost destitute of work.'

A view from the Green, *c.* 1908.

Prior to the collapse of the industry there were often strikes, demonstrations and even riots. Before the 1824 repeal of the Combination Laws strikes were illegal, but the weavers made their discontent known. One notable event took place on the Green. The problem arose out of an unscrupulous master's use of a long warping bar, used to warp and spool a chain of yarn for the weavers. The effect of using an over-long bar was to produce a chain of yarn longer than average. As weavers were paid by the chain, this fraudulent practice worked to their detriment. The inventor of this fraud, Edward Jackson, went bankrupt and all his goods were sold. At his sale the weavers bought the bars, the pins of which were of an enormous circumference, and after the ceremony of a mock trial, where the bars were arraigned for being invaders of the public peace, they were sentenced to be burnt forthwith, which was accordingly done, amid much merriment, on Uley Green.

One singular fact about Uley is the almost total lack of building in the village between 1838 and the end of the First World War. The village experienced almost a century of stagnation and depopulation. Any photograph taken at the turn of the century could, with just a few differences, be a picture taken sixty years before. If anything, there was a net surplus of demolitions as against new buildings.

Two views looking down the Street. The top picture, of *c.* 1947, shows the Lower Crown on the left-hand side. The bottom picture was taken from outside the Lower Crown, *c.* 1920.

Let us leave the depressions of the nineteenth century to look at the descendants of those who did not emigrate. Both photographs on this page were taken exactly one century after the collapse of the local economy in 1837–8.

Two views of the Street. The top picture shows the Lamb Inn on the right, *c.* 1905. Note the leaded panes in the house on the right. This was the traditional form for windows in most local cottages and houses. The bottom picture shows a similar view taken from a position slightly further up the Street, *c.* 1930.

Left-hand page, top: This picture shows a class of Uley School in 1937. The teacher is Miss Nellie White. Back row, left to right: Austin Holder, Bill Bruton, Tom Pitts, Stan Fryer, John Watson, Frank Ford, Leslie Smith, Brian Barton and John Clifford. Second row: Gordon Thompson, Colin Hill, Ruby Allen, Dorothy Evans, Betty Brindle, Diana Powell, Doris Herbert, Alma Mills, Sheila Brown, Margaret Stinchcombe, Midge Dolbear, Derek Niblett and Dennis Haddrell. Front row: Doreen Jenkins, Fred Athey, Dolly Bloodworth, Mary Ward and Mick Smith.

Left-hand page, bottom: The proud winners of the Berkeley Hospital Cup in 1937/8. Back row, left to right: C. Price, L. Price, H. Hurcombe, J. Bennett, H. Herbert, E. Woodward and J. Herbert. Front row: C. Herbert, T. Holister, M. Smith (mascot), V. Bennett and R. Cox.

Two views taken further down the Street, looking up towards the church. The top picture is of *c.* 1906, the bottom view, *c.* 1925. In one of the handloom weaver's cottages going up the Street lived John Ford who, until about 1890, continued to work at his loom, many years after all other weaving was factory based. He worked on kerseymeres, which he supplied to Cam Mills. Once, when delivering his woven cloth to the mill by donkey cart, A.B. Winterbotham, the owner, who was obviously not worried about mincing his words, told him that he ought to be stuffed and put in a glass case as a curiosity. John Henry Blunt refers to Ford in 1877, saying that at that time there were just two looms working in the parish, that of an old man (Ford) and his wife.

The King's Head. The top picture is of *c.* 1905, the bottom picture, with the Kingscote Hounds, *c.* 1935. The hounds were kennelled at the Weavers, now the Uley Brewery.

Whitecourt Chapel, *c.* 1910. Notice the alignment of the junction, the main direction of the road from Cam and Coaley being towards Whitecourt rather than down Fop Street. Whitecourt Chapel was built in 1791, a high point in the history of the Nonconformist movement. The population of the village was significant, and many of those involved in the clothing trade would have preferred the services to those of the Anglican church.

A view of Uley from the Bury, *c.* 1910.

Two views of the crossroads. The top picture is taken from the site of the sheep dip looking up towards Coombe House, an elegant early-eighteenth-century house built, rather suprisingly, of sandstone. By the side of the sheep dip is the site of Jackson's Mill, the same Jackson as mentioned on page 24. The lower view shows the crossroads from Dursley, looking up towards the King's Head with the Shears Inn on the right-hand side.

Two views from the crossroads looking up towards the King's Head. The top picture is of *c.* 1920, the bottom picture, *c.* 1930. The Shears Inn is on the right-hand side.

Marsh Mills. The top picture shows the saw mill, *c.* 1905, the bottom picture shows the mill buildings on the opposite side of the mill pond, *c.* 1910. This mill was one of the last working cloth mills in Uley but ceased operation in the 1840s. All the buildings were part of the same mill complex. The top picture shows the louvred loft for drying cloth. In 1831 it was valued at £181, but after the collapse of the industry its value plummeted to £50 in 1838. It later became a saw mill and the combustibility of sawdust played no small part in the 1915 fire. The bottom picture is taken looking towards Smallpox Hill.

MARSH MILLS ULEY.

Marsh Mills. Two pictures taken following the disastrous fire of 13 August 1915 which totally destroyed the main mill buildings.

Lampern Hill, *c.* 1910.

The Smith Family. This incredible picture was taken at the same time as the photograph on pages 2 and 3. It shows twenty-three members of the family at Lampern Quarry, *c.* 1885. These pictures show that great thought went into the general composition and individual poses, especially that of the Chaplinesque character in the foreground with his bowler and tie and umbrella.

A view of the village, *c.* 1905. Note the lack of trees on the hills and the remaining buildings of Sheppard's Mill on the right-hand side.

Whitecourt. A view from the fields beside the top of Lampern Hill, *c.* 1910. On the left is Stoutshill, built by William Halfpenny in 1743 in the Gothic 'Strawberry Hill' style for a wealthy clothier by the name of Gyde.

From Uley there were two roads to Dursley. The high road went via Shadwell and past Sheephouse Farm to end at the top of Woodmancote. The other road took, in the main, the same course as the present road, but from Uley it went via Whitecourt, behind Angeston, past Newbrook Farm and Wresden to join the current road nearer to Dursley. The 'turnpiking' of the road in the eighteenth century created the basis of the road we know today. Our tour takes the old road past Sheephouse Farm to Woodmancote. The view above probably shows part of this old road in the Shadwell/ Elcombe region.

Dursley

BELL&CASTLE HOTEL

Commercial & Old Posting House

PEPWORTHS SERIES.

A view looking down Whiteway Hill, *c.* 1900.
The previous two pages show Parsonage Street, *c.* 1910, looking towards the Hollies.

Woodmancote Farm, c. 1888. The farmhouse was built in 1869 on the site of a larger old house. The walled garden on the left was the landscaped gardens and kitchen gardens of the Rangers. This photograph was taken very shortly after the Rangers owner, Mr F.J. Searancke, had caused several cottages opposite the New Inn to be demolished to create space for his garden. This photograph was probably taken on a Monday as it is obviously washday for the occupants of Holywell Cottages, built in 1820 by Thomas Tippetts of New Mills as cottages for his handloom weavers.

These two pictures show Woodmancote Nursery Gardens, *c.* 1915. The nursery gardens were started in the mid-nineteenth century by Robert Smith, later bought by John Morse and then passed to his son Edward Morse. It later became Brinicombe & Son, nurserymen and seedsmen. When closed it was used for vehicle maintenance by J.H. Grange & Son, and later became Cousins's garage. The top picture has a backdrop of Rosebery Terrace, built in 1901 by Robert Ashton Lister to let to his workers at 4 shillings a week for three bedrooms, 6 shillings for five bedrooms. The terrace was named after Philip Archibald Primrose, fifth Earl Rosebery, a Liberal politician admired by Ashton Lister and just two years his junior.

St Mark's church, *c.* 1900. The church was built in 1844 as a chapel of ease for the parish church; its churchyard became the official parish burial ground after the closure of the parish churchyard for burial in the middle of the nineteenth century.

The Vizard Almshouses, next to St Mark's churchyard, built and endowed in the early nineteenth century by Henry Vizard for three poor men and three poor women. This photograph was taken in 1968, shortly before demolition.

The corner of Fort Lane, Woomancote, before and after demolition. The top picture was taken in 1967, the bottom picture in 1968.

Two views of Cleverly's garage in 1965. Frederick Percy Cleverly was one of the earliest motor engineers in Dursley, operating from Woodmancote from the 1920s onwards.

The top of Bull Pitch, c. 1908. Until the very early part of the nineteenth century, the manors of Dursley and Woodmancote were separated by a large triangular-shaped open green which was exactly the ground covered by the houses in this photograph. This green was open on both the Uley Road and Woodmancote sides, with a large chestnut tree at the upper end, near to which stood the pillory and stocks for the manor of Woodmancote. On the east side of the green, at the corner of the road to Uley, stood a large, rough-cast old house belonging to the town doctor, Dr Fry, with surgery and dispensary. This house was taken down around 1820 and the ashlar-fronted house with shutters built by Dr Fry in its place.

The Green was used for camp by horse soldiers who were called to Dursley to quell riots, especially the weavers' disturbances of 1825. It was also used for wild beast shows, travelling shows and Wombell's menagerie. It was closed off and built upon during 1830, the year of William IV's accession.

These two pictures are both *c*. 1904, and show the Bull Inn, a tied house of Elvy's Brewery. These houses and the inn were all built about 1830.

Members of the Francillon family with chauffeur outside the Bull Inn, *c.* 1910, with F.R. Francillon sitting on the running board. Note that Godsell's have acquired Elvy's Brewery. The Francillons lived opposite the Bull in a house demolished to make way for Hillside Court. The house had been built by Edward Bloxsome in 1804.

Celebrations at the top of Bull Pitch, *c.* 1936, with the Bull Inn in the background.

The circus comes to town. An elephant in Bull Pitch advertising the arrival of the circus, *c.* 1935. The circus came by train, and I recall in the 1950s being taken down Long Street by my sister and standing outside Lloyds Bank with many other youngsters to watch the elephants being brought up the street in procession, trunk holding tail, making their way to the recreation ground.

The New Dursley Fire Brigade in the coach house yard of Stanthill House, *c.* 1890. The brigade was reorganized in 1879, and proudly announced itself ready for active service at any destination within four minutes! The coach house was built on the opposite side of the Uley Road to Dr Fry's house, adjacent to the footpath leading down to Goody Mead.

Charles Hancock outside his first shop in Bull Pitch, *c*. 1890.

A view down Bull Pitch in 1907. Charles Hancock's shop is on the right-hand side, with the roller blind down. The wall on the left enclosed F.R. Francillon's house. This house was built on the site of three old cottages in 1804. In one of these old cottages, two hundred years ago, lived William Jenkins, a small deformed man who, being unable to walk, was placed daily in a chair outside his door with crockery and earthenware arranged around him for sale. On occasion, he would ride about the countryside selling his earthenware from a low cart on which was tied a chair to which he was securely fastened.

The bottom of Bull Pitch, *c.* 1914, showing the cottages on the bank opposite the monkey puzzle tree which can be seen on the previous page next to Charles Hancock's shop. The shop had been demolished by this time, and the railings of the house that replaced it can just be seen on the right-hand side of the photograph. As an aside – and as there is room on this page – a piece of useless information. The monkey puzzle tree is really the Chile pine. It was first introduced to Britain from South America in 1795 and was given its nickname by Victorian visitors to Pencarrow in Cornwall who, when shown one of the trees which had been grown for a novelty, recoiled in near disbelief, saying 'well, it would puzzle a monkey to climb that.' The building below the cottages on the left was the fire station, shown more clearly from the front on the next page. At the corner of Silver Street leading to the Broadwell was the original shop of Mr Walters, baker and confectioner. This shop and the one next to it have since been demolished to widen the entrance to the Broadwell.

The Dursley Fire Brigade outside the fire station in Bull Pitch. They are all decorated up, and other flags are evident. This was probably for Queen Victoria's Diamond Jubilee in 1897.

The Dursley Fire Brigade in 1964, shortly before moving to the new station in Castle Street. From left to right: Oscar Stanley, Charles Burnham, E. Pullen, Fred Arthurs, Len Frost, Tony Frost, Basil Allen, Ken Harnden, Bert Webb, -?-, Doc Billett, L. Frost, M. Bowen.

Two views of Henlow House. The top picture, showing Mr and Mrs Adams outside, was taken before the extension was built in 1900. The bottom picture shows the house transformed, with a young Cecil Adams standing on the lawn.

At the bottom of Bull Pitch we turn into the Broadwell and the top of Water Street, earlier known as 'Back Street'. The powerful springs here provided the power for the earliest mills, only being replaced by steam in the early nineteenth century. This was the centre of the medieval town and in my opinion holds the key to the future success of Dursley. It needs a sensible planning authority with a coherent plan, imaginative developers, co-operative owners and civic will to turn this corner of the town into a street to be proud of. Instead we have twentieth-century mess, nineteenth-century industrial squalor and indifference.

This photograph shows the Broadwell as it was in 1959 before the general clearance and tidying in this corner. A brave attempt, and well worth while, but much too little. The building on the right was the Broadwell Tavern at the turn of the century. It is a medieval building, and would have comprised one large room at one end, open to the roof, with a hole to let out smoke and, at the other end, a floor for sleeping quarters with a kitchen below.

Right-hand page, top: Frost damage led to the collapse of the end wall of the Tavern in 1983. This picture illustrates well the medieval building technique of limestone rubble and clay. The foundations are Cotswold stone boulders, and on this rubble stone is built using soft malleable clay as a form of mortar.

Right-hand page, bottom left: The budgerigar flight in 1959. This house was built in 1715 by the Cam Meeting Presbyterian minister, Joseph Twemlow, as a weekday school, and was in use as such until 1887. The income from land in the Berkeley Vale that once supported the school is now used to give grants to children of Free Church parents who attend centres of further education – the Twemlow Trust.

Right-hand page, bottom right: The same house in 1968 following a devastating fire.

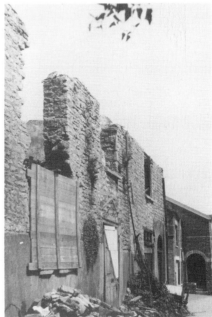

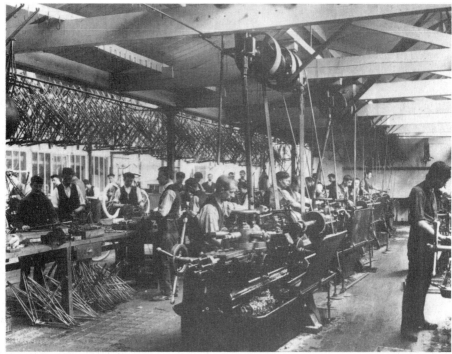

The two small mills further down the street were worked by James and John Howard in the early nineteenth century. The Upper Mill was a fulling and gigging mill, where the cloth was pounded with large, power-driven wooden hammers in a large trough with a mixture of fuller's earth and human urine, then rinsed through with water. The gigs were engines used for raising the knap of the cloth after fulling. Most of this mill still stands. In the 1870s it became a pin mill, worked by J. Hemmings, and at the turn of the century the mill formed part of Mikael Pedersen's cycle works. The photograph shows the inside of the works *c.* 1900.

A view from Chestal, *c.* 1900, showing the mill buildings at the lower end of Water Street.

This fascinating photograph of 1882, or just before, views Dursley from a position on the hillside between the top of Drake Lane and the drive leading up to Chestal. Raglan House can be seen on the right-hand side, and to the left of the church can be seen Howard's Upper Mill. The group of buildings in the foreground are particularly interesting as they were either demolished or otherwise incorporated in Ashton Lister's earlier phases of development. The Union Workhouse can be seen in the background.

The path to Yellow Hundred as built by W.J. Phelps. A photograph of *c.* 1905.

Taking the right-hand turn towards the bottom of Water Street you enter Hogg Leaze Lane, passing the site of the Bell and Apple Tree public house, and head along Yellow Hundred towards the Goody Mead, a path leading back up to Woodmancote and coming out at the top of Bull Pitch between Woodmancote Court and Stanthill House coach house. Passing the bottom of Goody Mead along the stream, you head towards Ferney Hill and the site of Thomas Tippetts's New Mills. It was at these mills that the riots of 1825 were started by the introduction of new machinery. A local magistrate, Mr Baker of Uley, sent to the War Office and a troop of the 12th Lancers was sent to Dursley. After their tour of duty they were followed respectively by the 2nd Dragoon Guards, the 4th Royal Irish and the 3rd Dragoon Guards until the end of the troubles.

The path beside the stream was built by W.J. Phelps at about the same time as Chestal House was built in 1852. The Phelps's ancient family house was taken down at this same time. It stood where the lodge and driveway lead up to the present house, about one hundred yards to the east of the Priory. Phelps's Mill stood to the east of the old house, opposite the bottom of Water Street. When Chestal was built another driveway was put in leading past Ferney Hill towards Uley Road, with another lodge built by the roadside. Opposite this lodge stood some cottages built in 1815 by John Taylor, a carpenter from Chalford. Afterwards he built a large house next door which has recently been demolished to make room for a new block of flats. Taylor later converted his workshops into a public house, and it is on this site that the present Carpenters Arms stands.

Left-hand page, top: The Lower Mill was the first factory of Robert Ashton Lister. He started work from the mill in 1867. The premises were rented for £6 per year which included the privilege of using the stream-driven mill wheel for four hours daily. This picture is taken from an upstairs window in Raglan House and the Lower Mill can be seen on the left, with other Lister buildings in the background.

Left-hand page, bottom: This 1955 photograph of Dursley was taken from the top of the Priory garden, and shows more or less the same area as the view of seventy years earlier on page 57, with Lister buildings covering most of the lower Long Street area.

Ferney Hill, and the site of Thomas Tippetts's Mill, *c.* 1904.

The Priory, known in the nineteenth century as Townsend House.

Returning back along Yellow Hundred and past the Goody Mead we come to the Priory. The gardens in the picture to the left were previously covered by the yard of the Phelps's ancient family house. The owner of the Priory in the late nineteenth century was Frederick Vizard, and the gentleman in the boat may well be Vizard, with his wife looking on. Note the gardener on the right with an early lawn-mower. The lawn-mower was invented in 1830 by Edwin Budding, for some years a Dursley resident, living in May Lane and working for George Lister, Ashton Lister's father. The land for the garden in this picture of *c.* 1870 was presumably purchased by the then owner of the Priory from W.J. Phelps.

The photograph above is of Howard's Mill, *c.* 1900. There were a number of mills which at one time or another were operated by the Howard family. This mill had nothing to do with Howard's Upper Mill or Lower Mill. This mill stood at the bottom of Long Street in the area now covered by a Lister-Petter car park. The Rack Field, now housing a town car park, can be seen behind. This ancient cloth mill with mill pond in front was worked by John Howard in the early nineteenth century. It was acquired by Edward Gazard in the 1860s when he moved his carpentry, blacksmith and building business down from the site now covered by the Dursley Garage. The mill was bought by Ashton Lister in 1894 and demolished to make way for Lister's Churn Works some seven or eight years later. This photograph shows that the mill had great character. If it had survived until now it would undoubtedly be a listed building and a tourist attraction. This is an example of how Dursley's early commercial success has devastated our inheritance. In the foreground can be seen the gas-lit lane leading to the railway station.

Dursley

In Drake Lane, on the site now covered by the offices of Lister-Petter which replaced the offices burnt down in 1983, stood Rock House, built by Edward Gazard in 1865. The photograph above must have been taken from an upstairs window of the Towers, some time betwen 1897 and 1900, probably 1897 when the Towers was being built. Rock House is shown centre bottom. On the right is Edward Gazard's workshops, occupied in 1897 by J. Peake & Co., timber merchants. Other points of particular interest in this photograph are Robert Ashton Lister's first factory (the mill with the tall

chimney to the left of the picture), the Pedersen works (the mill behind Lister's in this view), the
workhouse at the top of Union Street, seen behind the church, and finally, the Chantry in Long Street,
now the Lister Social Club. One feature that unfortunately cannot be seen is the long mill pond which
was between Rock House and Howard's Mill. This mill pond later became the town swimming pool
and was subsequently covered by Lister's sheep shear works.

This interesting photograph was taken from the Rack Field around 1900. It shows Howard's Mill on the right-hand side and Rock House above the mill, faced by the handsome laurel hedge of the Priory on to Drake Lane. The Towers has just been completed and Dursley railway station can be seen on the left-hand side in the foreground. The Rack Field was so called as it was the drying ground for cloth manufactured at the mill. The field would have been covered by timber frames called 'tenters', and the cloth would be stretched across these and held by 'tenterhooks'. Another rack field was across the valley, on the ground covered by Rock House and the Towers.

The source of the famous Dursley tufa was somewhere at the bottom of Long Street on the same side of the street as Howard's Mill, probably just above the mill where other springs feed into the River Cam. The bed of rock may have extended beneath the Cam to where Rock House stood. Could this be how the house was given its name?

Dursley railway station, *c*. 1865, with an early 'Dursley Donkey', Midland Railway 0–4–2 number 202.

Dursley railway station, *c*. 1962, with one of the last passenger trains. The guard is Mr Edward Spilsbury.

The Dursley Donkey, *c.* 1857. This 0–4–0ST locomotive was built in 1856, probably by Stothert, Slaughter & Co. of Bristol, and was used by the contractor who built the Dursley branch line. The engine later became Midland Railway locomotive number 156. This photograph was probably taken just outside the station in Dursley with the Rack Field in the background. This photograph is undoubtedly the earliest picture in the book.

The Bristol to Gloucester railway bypassed Dursley, keeping to a more economic line in the Severn valley. Dursley businessmen who had seen the Stroud area prosper from cheap transport via canal and railway decided to finance their own railway company. Using second-hand rails and chairs from the Midland Railway, the Dursley and Midland Junction Railway opened to traffic on 25 August 1856. It lost money to begin with, and the company was sold to the Midland Railway in 1860, the original shareholders losing more than half of their investment. The branch line later made a profit for the Midland Railway Company.

Dursley railway station, *c.* 1902. After 106 years, passenger services came to an end at Dursley on 10 September 1962 – and I was one of those passengers! A sentimental journey, with the train packed to the luggage racks with enthusiasts, saying goodbye to the 'donkey'. Goods services continued until 1 November 1966, but the last breath was drawn on 13 July 1970 when Lister's closed their private siding.

Evacuees from Harwich School arriving at Dursley station in 1940.

Dursley railway station in 1965. The passengers have gone, the trees have gone and Lister's works have encroached. Very soon the station is to disappear and another part of Dursley committed to the history book.

The station yard, with Lister's shearing works on the right-hand side, *c.* 1920. These buildings covered the ancient mill pond.

The same buildings in 1968 with the addition of a first floor for offices.

An aerial view, *c.* 1929. Rock House is just about visible at the bottom of Drake Lane. This was demolished in 1937 to make way for R.A. Lister's new office block. The Rack Field can be seen in the middle of the picture. This was bought by Ashton Lister in 1908 and the part visible here is now the main factory car park. The Red Walk, leading to the site of George Harris's Lower Mill, later Dursley Brewery, is visible on the left of the picture. Below the Red Walk are the dried-up remains of the mill pond. The mill was about two hundred metres further west (left, out of picture) towards Upper Cam. The drive to Chestal is clearly visible but Drake Lane, leading to Upper Cam, is mainly hidden behind trees. Former First World War aircraft hangars are shown on the far left of the picture. These housed the Lister-Bruston Generating Set Department. They went up in flames a short while after this photograph was taken.

An aerial view of 1968, showing the 1937 office block destroyed in the 1983 fire. The new office block is built on the same site, and re-uses the steel structure of the 1937 building. The Churn Works, shown centre bottom in this photograph, were destroyed in the same fire. The intensity of the heat sent fireballs across the road, engulfing the works which stood on the site of Howard's Mill shown on page 61.

The devastation caused by the fire of 1983. Preliminary demolition work is in progress to get the firm back in full running order.

A winter picture of the bottom of Long Street in 1957, with the Priory steps on the right-hand side.

The same view as shown on the previous page in 1965. The first phase of demolition has been completed and the stub of the next building is just visible on the left. The drying sheds of Champion's Works are visible in front of the Rack Field, and the Lamb Inn sign can be seen on the right, next to the Priory.

A 1959 view up Long Street, with the physiotherapy clinic on the left-hand side. There is a 'For Sale' sign in front of the old Reliance Works.

A proud picture. A fine photograph, although unfortunately damaged at the top. The Reliance Works were the site of J.B. Champion's business. In the 1880s this was the manufacture of ropes, twines, sacks, matting, sail cloths and saddlery. The *British Universal Directory* of 1792 mentions one Samuel Champion of Dursley, saddler, so the business was long established. Champion's later developed from matting into carpet manufacture and had a larger factory in Boulton Lane, taking the site of Elvy's Brewery. This photograph is of *c.* 1905. The bottom picture is *c.* 1895.

The same view, taken a little further down Long Street outside what had been the Crown Inn up to this point. The licence was transferred to the next building up the street. A rare view of the houses at the bottom of Long Street on the right, the site later covered by Lister's offices. This picture, *c.* 1908, shows the Co-operative Stores prior to their moving to the Parsonage Street site in 1910.

Long Street in 1959, showing Wintle's shop still trading after seventy years. The shop was built about 1882 by Messrs Wintle Brothers after clearing away some ancient cottages. The building that was until recently the Crown Inn has had a face-lift or, to be more precise if comparing it with previous pictures, a face let-down.

Long Street Court during demolition in 1960.

Long Street Court and the front of the Reliance Works in 1960. Part of the back of the building was called Blackwell's Court after an owner of that name some two hundred years ago. Before becoming the Reliance Works this site was Dursley Old Brewery, owned by a Mr Young, later by Frederick Vizard and, by the mid-nineteenth century, Mr Carter. In this brewery were three large casks named 'Faith', 'Hope' and 'Charity'. The Golden Hart, now the Conservative Club, was owned by Mr Young and was a tied house to this brewery.

The home of J.W. Giddings, standing outside with his wife, *c.* 1910. Giddings was in business with William Hancock until at least 1931, after which the business became C.A. Giddings and Company. This house was at one time a public house, the White Hart.

Oh dear! Whatever happened to those beautiful medieval buildings? A photograph of 1969 after the building of Bailey's factory. It is inconceivable that demolition would have been allowed if we were facing the same situation today. It is unfortunate that these buildings could not have lasted another thirty years and been protected by a more sympathetic understanding of townscape and the environment.

The Market Place as seen from Long Street in 1959. The building immediately on the right was the site of the New Inn. The landlord in the 1830s was Sam Trotman, a trumpeter in the Dursley Yeomanry. It was sold by his daughter to Berkeley Wathen Bloxsome about 1840 who demolished it and built the present building on the site. Opposite was the Dursley branch of W.H. Smith. This is now part of the Conservative Club with a new 'old' facade. The site of the main part of the club, next door up, was the Golden Hart, and the passageway next to it leading to the churchyard was Golden Hart Entry.

A view from exactly the same position some sixty years earlier.

Edith C. Hancock outside her milliner's shop in Long Street, the shop shown on the right-hand side of the previous pictures. She ran this shop through the 1920s and 1930s. In this view of *c.* 1929 note the children in the upstairs window. One of these may have been Roy, Edith's son, who died during the post-war poliomyelitis epidemic.

The Market Place, *c.* 1900, with Wilkes's Drapery on the right-hand side.

Two views of the Market Place, the top picture of *c.* 1900, the bottom picture taken during demolition of the old police station and magistrates court in 1959.

Two views of the Market Place some thirty years apart. The top picture is of *c*. 1908, the bottom picture, 1938. No major changes but a few subtle differences: church gates, Wilkes's shop and the telephone box.

The parish church, *c.* 1897, before the new clock was installed slightly lower down the tower. The church originally had a spire but this collapsed on 7 January 1699 while the bells were being rung with the loss of several lives. The present tower was built in 1709.

The dedication of the War Memorial Gates, Armistice Day, 11 November 1922; an important day for the town. This view shows London House on the left, looking towards Silver Street. This house was completely refaced in 1840, and the shop and house front taken back several feet to make more room in the Market Place, or 'Bull Ring' as it was anciently known. The bull ring name came from the fact that a large iron ring was let into the centre of the road for tethering bulls for the explicit purpose of baiting. Until 1840, the principal entrance to the churchyard was from the top of Silver Street. In exchange for the ground given up in the Market Place, Messrs Hurndall and Son, drapers, were given the land that comprised this entrance, and they built the small shop shown on page 110. Other houses were demolished in 1840 to make the space now covered by the present war memorial church gates and driveway.

Left-hand page, top and bottom: The Market Place, *c.* 1887. These pictures were taken from the first floor of the house in Silver Street overlooking the Market Place. There are several pictures in this sequence and two are reproduced here. The top one shows the start of the procession. The enlargement below shows part of a banner and good examples of the costumes which helps to date the photographs. The straw boaters and the striped cap are typical of 1885–90. This could be a celebration of Queen Victoria's Golden Jubilee of 1887.

A modern view of London House in a photograph of 1956, some three years prior to demolition and the general opening of the Market Place, and the exposing of the church to general view for the first time ever. London House had been a drapers' premises for centuries. In the 1840s it belonged to Messrs Hurndall, later becoming Troughton's, and was, until the middle of this century, Kemp's.

The police station and magistrates courts in 1959, immediately before demolition. A view from Parsonage Street.

The police station in 1959, viewed from the Knapp.

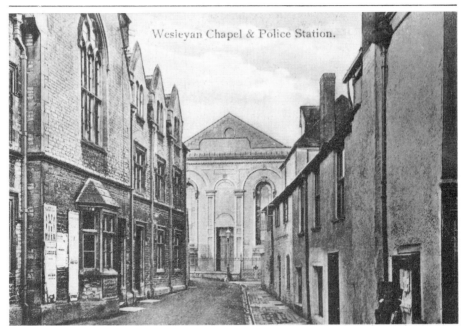

Wesleyan Chapel & Police Station.

The Knapp viewed from the Market Place, *c.* 1905. The police station and courts on the left were built in 1865 on the site of the Lamb Inn. The frontage of the Lamb had been about three or four feet back from the frontage shown in this photograph, and in front of it were butchers' shambles. In this space were vertical posts to hold the butchers' stalls on market days. These were later removed, allowing space for bay windows to be placed in the inn before that finally disappeared in 1864. In the space on the extreme left of the picture, leaning against the Lamb Inn, was a large blindhouse – the town lock-up. To the right of the inn, further up from the shambles, were the stocks and pillory. Convicted petty thiefs were dragged from the lock-up and past the shambles to suffer their sentence of ridicule.

The small house immediately on the right of this picture was the Boot Inn. By the mid-nineteenth century this had become a grocer's shop, and later became Wilkes. The licence for the Boot was transferred to Silver Street (see page 108).

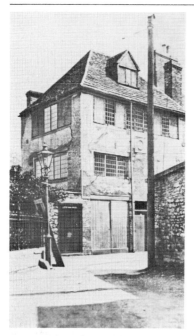

The Knapp, *c.* 1947. The wall on the right was demolished in 1959, together with the police station and courts, and the present road built, stage one being a one-way system starting from the Castle Farm entrance (now the gap between Barclays Bank and the Job Centre) and leading towards the Market Place. The name 'Knapp' means small hill, in this case the steep ridge by the side of Castle Farm, now covered by car park and swimming pool.

A view from almost the same spot as the picture above, taken in 1964 after demolition and looking across to Parsonage Street, showing the new one-way system with 'up' traffic still using Parsonage Street.

Two views of the new fire station site, the top picture taken in late summer, 1964, the bottom picture in early 1965. The new one-way system can be clearly seen here, the road winding round from Castle Farm entrance. The hillock of the Knapp is in the background, its fragrant lime trees lining the right-hand side of the pathway bordering the Rack Field. County planning was not very bright here. Would it not have made sense to have had the fire station at Sandpits and the new police station here?

Rednock

Di

Captain George Augustus Graham with two of his Irish wolfhounds, *c.* 1904. Graham was born in Bath in 1833 and saw army service in the 107th Bengal Infantry. After his army career, which included the Indian Mutiny of 1857, he retired to Dursley in 1865, buying the Oaklands Estate from George Harris. The estate was also referred to as 'Oatlands' or the 'Ten Acres'. Graham came from a wealthy family, as retirement at thirty-two might imply. He renamed the estate 'Rednock', and for several years I have been trying to find out why. One possibility is that the land behind, running by the side of the Lower Mill pond, was known as the 'Red Walk', and Rednock might have been the vernacular dialect corruption of this which Graham decided to adopt. One other possibility which occurs to me is that with a surname such as Graham, his family may have been Scottish or Irish, and that with 'nock' being a Gaelic place name denoting a hill, this may have been the name of a family estate or some other home connection.

Graham rescued the Irish wolfhound breed from extinction and his efforts were recognised in tributes from the Irish Wolfhound Club in 1904. Apparently, he bred remaining examples of wolfhounds and deerhounds for more than forty years to produce the breed that is recognized today. All Irish wolfhounds descend from his dogs. He died in 1909, all local shops were shut for the funeral, and the town turned out to mourn its leading citizen. The house and estate was sold to Robert Ashton Lister in 1910.

Dursley Secondary School, *c.* 1930. Ashton Lister sold the house and estate to the County Council in 1921 and it became Dursley Secondary School, with Ernest Barrett as headmaster. The school became Dursley Grammar School in 1947.

Rednock Drive, *c.* 1920

Kingshill Road, *c.* 1910. The raised pathway on the right was made from soil and rubble excavated from the back of houses at the top of Silver Street adjoining the churchyard in 1840 (see page 85).

Dursley Recreation Ground, *c.* 1960. The police station has been demolished but the Bell and Castle and parts of Castle Farm are still standing, as are the shops that adjoined the post office, where the current road now cuts through.

The Pike House, *c*. 1880.

The wheelwrights yard of J.H. Lewis, *c*. 1900, viewed from just outside the Pike House, a site now covered by the garage.

The Dursley Garage, *c.* 1925. This had been the wheelwrights yard of J.H. Lewis, and before that the timber yard of Edward Gazard before he moved to the bottom of Long Street (see page 61). Further down towards the town were thatched cottages and a blacksmiths forge. These were demolished in 1865 and John Harding built his Agricultural Implement Warehouse on the site and Spring Villa adjoining. The site of Harding's warehouse was the home of the *Gazette* until the 1960s when the main works moved to Long Street, followed in the late 1970s by the offices.

The Dursley Garage. The top picture is of *c.* 1925, the bottom picture 1968, the days of Vespas and parkas.

The crescent, built by Edward West in the 1820s, opposite the Tabernacle. His own house was next door, now covered by the Midland Electricity showrooms. This house was taken down and the present premises built on the site in the middle of the nineteenth century by West's son-in-law, Edward Gazard, with workshops and a timber yard behind. Edward Gazard seems to have had timber yards all over Dursley!

The junction of May Lane, c. 1946. The corner premises were the Co-op café, the next shop up being Harry Pegler and Son, butchers. The main Co-operative stores moved to this Parsonage Street site in 1910 from their previous premises in Long Street.

May Lane in 1968. The site on the left has been derelict since demolition of the corner café and a row of cottages several years before.

Parsonage Street, looking back towards the Hollies, *c.* 1910. Gazard's building can be seen in this view, as can the façade of the farm buildings that preceded the Co-operative Stores. The Hollies, a farmhouse built in 1733, was the residence and stables of J.M. Buston, a haulier and contractor.

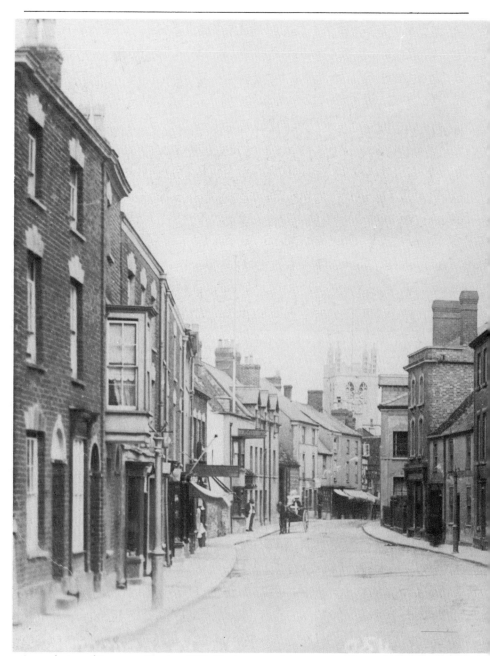

A superb view of Parsonage Street, *c.* 1905. The houses and shops on the left were built between 1815 and 1820, and the nearest building on the left became the town's first telephone exchange. These first two buildings were demolished in 1963 to make way for the second phase of the ring road in Castle Street. The farm building on the right was demolished very shortly after this photograph was taken,

and the Dursley branch of the Cainscross and Ebley Co-operative Stores built on the site. The corner building in May Lane was demolished together with other low cottages leading up May Lane in about 1960.

Parsonage Street, *c.* 1950, a Remembrance Parade, with my grandfather, Harold Mayo, carrying the British Legion standard.

Success to our volunteers! The Dursley Contingent of the Royal Gloucestershire Hussars riding through Parsonage Street. They formed part of the 3rd Company of the 1st Battalion, Imperial Yeomanry during the Boer War. Wishing them success would seem to indicate that they are about to depart. If so, this would date this photograph as January 1900.

Left-hand page, top: The Bell and Castle Hotel, c. 1900. This site is now occupied by Barclays Bank. Note the entrance to Castle Farm and farm buildings on the left-hand side. Until 1959 cows were still being herded down Parsonage Street for milking. It is hard to imagine cows being herded past Barclays Bank now, only thirty-two years later! The licensee was the father of Rowland Vigus, and Rowland started his garage business in buildings to the rear of the hotel before moving to May Lane. His May Lane business changed hands and became Murray's Motors. The horses and carriage in this photograph was the courtesy coach collecting and taking residents to the station.

Parsonage Street, *c.* 1905. The building immediately on the left was originally the White Lion Inn. By the middle of the nineteenth century this had become Mr Blackney's carriage building shop, and by the end of the century A.T. Walters and Son, bakers and confectioners. The building on the right was the post office at the time of this photograph, and remained so until the new post office was built in the 1930s. It was built by Edward Bloxsome in 1840 as the Dursley branch of the National Provincial Bank. Previously on the site was an apothecary's shop belonging to Thomas Gregory, who is listed in *British Universal Directory* of 1792.

Two views of Parsonage Street approximately twenty years apart. The top picture is of *c.* 1938, the bottom picture 1959. Note the variety of subtle changes between these two, and the previous three photographs.

The Star Supply Stores and the Cotswold Café, Parsonage Street. The premises changed from the Star Grocery Company to the International Stores some time between 1935 and 1939. This photograph is of *c*. 1934.

The Market Place as seen from the top of Silver Street, *c.* 1900. The corner of Kemp's shop can be seen on the right and the fire brigade ladder can be seen strung under the Market House.

Hill Court House, with Charles and Stuart Hancock outside. This had been Hawker & Sons, 'purveyors of all the primest and best quality meat. Families waited upon for orders daily.' It was later to become Baxters. See the same premises on page 109.

Silver Street, *c.* 1900, but definitely before 1903 as the Star at the bottom was demolished and rebuilt in that year and this photograph shows the old building. The Boot Inn had previously been on the corner of the Market Place and the Knapp (see page 89), but when this was closed the licence was transferred to these premises in Silver Street.

The Victoria Hall was the main meeting place and theatre house in Dursley; it was also a coffee house, as the sign advertises, and a temperance hotel. The temperance movement, campaigning against the evils of drink, was at its zenith in the 1880s, and great efforts were made to find places of wholesome entertainment away from public houses. This later became the town's first cinema, starting off with silent movies.

Silver Street, *c.* 1918. The Victoria Theatre has now become the town's first cinema.

Silver Street in 1959. This picture shows the remains of the block of buildings that faced the Market House. By 1969 further road widening had seen all of these buildings demolished down to the church steps.

The Church Lads Brigade on parade, *c.* 1911. The Boot Inn had closed about 1910 and the premises taken over by George Witchell, tobacconist and confectioner, who continued in this business until about 1937. Kemp's owned the small shop bearing their name in this picture as well as the more substantial buildings facing the Market Place. This is the shop referred to on page 85 that was built by Mr Hurndall on land given to him, in exchange for several feet of frontage in the Market Place, at the original entrance to the churchyard. The very tall house on the right of this photograph is London & Manchester House, shown on the page opposite as it was forty years before.

London & Manchester House, *c.* 1870. To the right of this building, but set back slightly to the extent that it is out of view in this photograph, was another smaller house. Beyond this was the churchyard entrance and steps, with an archway overhead. The door shown in the shadows on the right is blocked in today but, standing on the present churchyard steps, it is possible to see where it was.

Silver Street, c. 1910. To the right of this can be seen the small, set-back house, with the arch over the churchyard entrance partially obstructed by the shop blind. This entrance was made in 1838 when the old parish workhouse was demolished. The workhouse stood exactly over the area of the steps and to each side, up to London & Manchester House on the west, and where the chemist's shop stands in the picture on page 113 to the east. An enlargment of part of this picture is also shown on page 114.

Silver Street in 1965, after the demolition of London & Manchester House together with the shops and houses on each end of it – and the church archway.

The workhouse that stood on this site was set back from the road with a flight of stone steps leading to the ground floor level which stood at the same height as the churchyard. The workhouse inmates broke stones for roadmending, but also made pins. A local businessman, Reuben Hill, speculated in the 1830s, in housebuilding, manufacturing and 'farming the poor' in pin manufacturing. Children of this time sang a ditty:

> Reuben Hill starved the poor
> To have a new brass knocker
> Put on his door.

Reuben Hill was the builder of Hill Square at the bottom of Gasworks Pitch (Kingshill Lane), which is named after him and not from the fact that it is on a hill.

Boulton Lane, October 1956, before demolition commences. The 'drill hall' is just visible half-way up the lane on the right-hand side. This was built in 1828 after dissension among dissenters! A great falling-out between local Nonconformists resulted in this chapel being built but services did not last for long before reconciliation arose between the warring parties. It then became the Nonconformist school until 1897 when the new school was built next to the Methodist chapel and it became the drill hall for the territorials, commencing in 1897 with the Dursley Company, the 2nd Volunteer Battalion of the Gloucestershire Regiment.

Two views of Boulton Lane. The top view is of 1956, the bottom during demolition in 1959.

The Boulton Lane celebrations to commemorate King Edward VII's coronation in 1902. From left to right: Walter Chester, Kate Large, Mrs Chester, Clara Ford, Tom Land, -?-, Ellen Hancock, Edward Higgins, Mrs Wood, Mrs Pepworth, Edward Wood, Betsy Cross, Elizabeth French, George Elliott, Mrs Morgan, Mrs Elliott, -?-, Mrs Higgins, Mrs Ann Cross, Louisa Hancock. This family photograph shows my grandmother, Louisa Sutton (née Hancock), her sister Ellen, and their grandmother, Betsy Cross.

The building on the right is the Cross Keys, on the left, Rose Cottage, and then a little further down, the drill hall. Just in view at the bottom of the road is the Star Inn in Silver Street. This was demolished and rebuilt in 1903. The factory on the right was Elvy's Brewery; the site was later developed as Champion's carpet works. In recent years it was the Bymack's furniture factory until demolition in 1987.

Above: The Slade at the junction of Union Street and Boulton Lane in 1956. Walking up the hill is my grandfather Joe Sutton. After a family difference, Joe left his Birmingham home in 1895 and walked to Uley to stay with his uncle, David Sutton, at Rockstowes.

Right-hand page, top left: Soldiers, including some Hancocks, outside the drill hall during the First World War.

Top right: My great-great-grandmother, Betsy Cross, at the back of Rose Cottage with three of my aunts, Joe's daughters, in the late autumn of 1913. In the background is the drill hall. The baby is Queenie Winifred May, standing is Mabel Emmie, and seated with doll is Elizabeth Poppy. Elizabeth (Bessy) died of diphtheria just a few weeks after this photograph was taken.

Gone! The drill hall demolished and awaiting clearance in 1959.

Looking down the Slade in 1959 during demolition. The evening sun is shining in the foreground from the path on the right leading up to Hill View. It was at Hill View that the celebrated murder of 1859 occurred, when Ellen Rutter cut her husband's throat. As a boy I often stayed in the room where the murder took place, and recall my cousin's glee in showing me the stains in the floorboards, under the rug. Thomas Rutter was first married to Betsy Cross's sister, Hannah Elliott. She died not long after giving birth to a son, Thomas junior. Rutter then married Ellen, already of bad character, and both she and Rutter were drunkards. On 7 August, in fear of her own life, she took the razor he kept under his pillow in order to threaten him and slit his throat.

Right-hand page, bottom left: Joseph with Mabel outside Hill View, *c.* 1912.

Right-hand page, bottom right: Louisa, seated centre, outside Hill View, with her sisters and brother, *c.* 1912. Top left, Ellen; top right, Winifred; front left, Gertrude; bottom left, Elizabeth. Standing at the back is the only boy, Arthur Hancock. All lived to a grand old age, especially Arthur who died in 1986 aged 100. In the background the form of the workhouse can just about be made out.

Right: Joseph and Louisa Sutton in the garden of Rose Cottage, Boulton Lane, on their wedding day, Christmas Day 1903.

The Union Workhouse, *c*. 1930, the view looking up the drive from the gateway on Union Street.

The Union Workhouse, another view in the same series of shots, this time showing the front door with Hermitage Wood as a backdrop.

The front of the Union Workhouse, looking over Hunger Hill to woodlands beyond.

The view looking down the front path towards the Slade. The flowers were pinks which were prepared and supervised by the workhouse master, Mr Wilson.

A view from the woods looking down on the workhouse and the town, *c.* 1904. The new union workhouses came about from the Poor Law Reform Acts of 1834 and 1836. Dursley Union Workhouse was built in 1837 using stone quarried in the hill behind, the stone being winched down with full buckets pulling up empty buckets. The new workhouse served a union of thirteen parishes around, the furthest being Kingswood. The old workhouse in Silver Street was then closed and demolished. The system came to an end in 1948 with the National Assistance Act, and this particular building was demolished in the mid 1950s.

In a troubled history, the most notorious event occurred in 1842 when an effigy of the master was paraded around the town in a public demonstration, sparked off by a violent quarrel between the master and matron over his behaviour with a female pauper. A girl of 12 who had run away for fear of being accused of stealing lace was brought back by her aunt and ultimately forced to tell the board how the master had sexually abused her four or five times and begun to beat her. The guardians, a weak and deficient lot, decided this was a case for the magistrates but offered no help and the master was allowed to resign, so the board avoided having to explain the circumstances to the Poor Law Commission.

This early photograph of Dursley is taken from the same spot as the photograph opposite, but some forty years earlier as it can be accurately dated to 1865. The old rectory is still standing (to the left of the Tabernacle in this picture) and it is known that most of the building was demolished in 1866. Spring Villa (now the home of the cricket club) has been built, which is known to have happened in 1865. Part of the workhouse can be seen on the right-hand side, especially one of the exercise yards with high walls for the segregation of the sexes, and of adults from children.

The row of cottages in Hill Road was built in 1815 by James Harding and subsequently named Harding's Row. They were colloquially known as 'pig-face row' as they had doors at the back only and no doors on to the street. These cottages were demolished in the 1950s and the car park in Hill Road stands on this spot. The chapel in Hill Road, now a garage, was built by Messrs Pocock, Pyer and Smith, Wesleyan Methodists from Bristol. It lasted only a short time as a chapel before falling into disuse. James Wood, a carpenter, built Underhill House next door in the 1820s, and subsequently used the chapel as a workshop.

The houses in May Lane, the Manse and Woodland Villa (now the Happy Pig), were also built in the mid 1820s and an old hedge and ditch removed and iron railings placed past the houses.

View from road up Stinchcombe, shewing Union, Dursley

Two views from the Broadway, both *c.* 1900. The top photograph shows the Union Workhouse and neat rows of vegetables maintained by the inmates. The Wesleyan minister's manse can be seen in the foreground. The bottom photograph shows a small corner of the workhouse garden and a view over the town, with Harding's Row centre foreground.

Stinchcombe Hill. Two views of early golf club houses at the beginning of the century. Attempts were made to enclose the hill in the early 1880s by the owners at the time, but public outrage at the loss of an amenity which had been enjoyed for centuries forestalled the enclosure. One argument used against enclosure was that the Rifle Volunteers would have nowhere to practice in readiness for any war that might occur!

General view of Dursley, *c.* 1902. This is a fascinating picture, enlarged from a collotype postcard, showing the town in the form in which it survived, by and large, until 1958. Thirty years of blight since then have destroyed many fine buildings and replaced them with utilitarian eyesores.

Dursley County Primary School is shown next to the Methodist church, and in front of the school is Castle Farm. To the left of the picture can be seen the racks of drying rugs, carpets and other woven materials from Champion's Reliance Works, possibly hanging on tenters if these were still used in

Dursley at this time. Champion's later built large drying sheds (see page 73). Chestal House can be seen top left, with Smallpox Hill as a backdrop. Between the church and the Priory it looks as if new building is taking place next to Ashton Lister's foundry.

Prospect Place, with the large gardens of the houses, can be seen on the right in the foreground and, at the back, Bull Pitch and Stanthill.

A view of the recreation ground from Westfield Wood, *c.* 1922. The bowling green on the left had been opened by Ashton Lister in 1920; the football pavilion built in 1925 is not yet evident.

A view of Dursley from Stinchcombe Hill just above Sheep Path Wood, *c.* 1900. The picture is too small to see great detail, but the three fields in the foreground can be seen before the development of the 1930s and 1960s. The area shown on the left is now covered by the top part of Olive Grove and St Davids Crescent, built in 1936. The field on the right is Beechwood Rise, built 1968, and nearer the town is Westfield, built 1962.

Westfield Lane, *c.* 1910. In the 1860s Westfield Lane was wide enough to drive horses and carriage up through Cockshoot Wood to Stinchcombe Hill. This photograph shows the land now covered by Olive Grove and St Davids Crescent. The building of the estate by Watts commenced in 1935, and the first phase was named Jubilee Road to celebrate George V's Silver Jubilee. Olive Grove and Lawrence Grove were named after members of the builder's family.

Two views of the Regal. The top picture is probably from 1953 as *Jeopardy*, starring Barbara Stanwyck, is being featured. The cinema and shops were built by L.J. Watts at the same time as the estate behind.

Upper Cam.

Kingshill House and a view of Upper Cam, taken from Stinchcombe Hill, *c.* 1910.

The name Kingshill comes from the King family who were living here between 1593 and 1702. Kingshill House was probably built by the Kings as a gabled mansion, and a directory of 1792 still lists one 'John King' among the principal gentry of the town, although it is not known if he still lived at the house at this time. It was then acquired by the Purnell family, and in the early nineteenth century was purchased by T.W. Richards from the estate of R.J. Purnell. In 1876 it was bought by Edwin Eyre, re-roofed, a totally new façade added and other extensions and alterations carried out. Most of the estate was bought by the Lister brothers in 1935. The house was conditionally given to the rural district council for the benefit of the town. Some land was given to the council for council housing with the primary intention of making housing available to Lister employees. The garden at the back of the house was given to the town as a memorial playground for children, the memorial being to the brothers' grandfather, Robert Ashton Lister, who had died in 1929. The rest of the land was sold for private housing development.

Cam & Coaley

UPPER CAM.

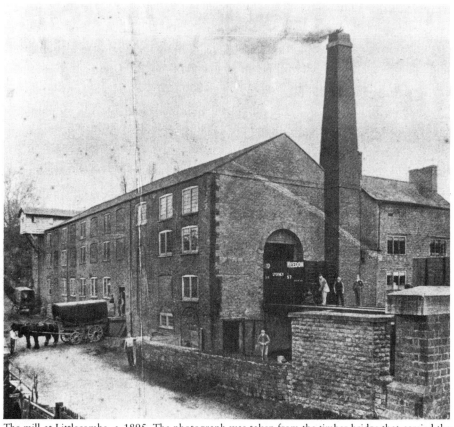

The mill at Littlecombe, *c.* 1895. The photograph was taken from the timber bridge that carried the railway line over the road. The bridge was demolished and the road raised and widened in 1970 after the railway closed. This mill was later converted to houses, and these too were demolished in the early 1970s to make the present Littlecombe entrance to Lister-Petter.

The picture on the previous two pages shows the cottages in Hopton Road at Noggin's Hole, or Teetotal Valley as it was called after the inclinations of one of the cottage occupants, a drinking man who took the pledge and saved sufficient money to build these cottages. Upper Cam church is in the background.

Cam Congregational church and schoolrooms, *c.* 1915.

Crossways, Upper Cam, *c.* 1925. This house, later a shop, but now a house once more, formed an island from the junction of Hopton Road and Spring Hill. Note how narrow the road is that turns into Hopton Road.

Cam Long Down as seen from Cam Peak, *c.* 1915. This postcard view was printed as a Christmas card, and shows the area used by the local rifle volunteers, the early territorials, as a rifle range. The poles may have been used to fly warning flags when shooting was taking place.

Cam Hopton School, *c.* 1910, with magnificent elm trees to the side. The house was built as a school with accommodation for a master with a bequest from Frances Hopton in 1738. A beautiful building with graceful proportions that is a credit to Cam and of great benefit to the street scene.

Cam station in 1960 shortly before closure. This was the only halt on the line between Dursley station and Coaley Junction. The picture was taken a little way beyond the level crossing gates looking towards the station. On the other side of the road to the gates was, and still is, the Railway Inn.

Hunt & Winterbotham's Cam Mills, *c.* 1930. Cam Hopton School is in the top right-hand corner of the photograph. It was to these mills that the poor broadweaver, John Ford of Uley, took his kerseymeres at the end of the nineteenth century – the last local exponent of the handloom weaving art.

Two views of Rowley, *c.* 1905. The top picture shows the rectory in Cam Pitch in the top left corner.

Two views of Chapel Street, looking towards High Street. The top picture is of *c.* 1905, the bottom picture slightly earlier, possibly *c.* 1900. Absalom or 'Appy' Ford is at work in his smithy. The Methodist chapel on the right was built in 1825.

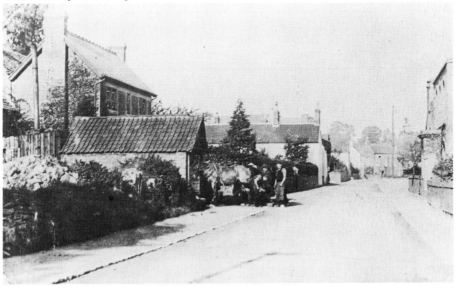

The junction of Chapel Street with the bottom of Cam Pitch. These two photographs are eleven years apart and show 'before' and 'after'. The top picture is of 1957, the bottom picture, 1968, after demolition on the corner.

More 'before' and 'after' views. The top picture is looking down Cam Pitch during demolition in 1957; the bottom picture, of 1968, shortly before the demolition of the old Co-operative Stores, shows the old manse of Cam Meeting. Note the mess of wires. Cam must suffer the blight of more street furniture litter in the form of road signs, telephone and electricity cables than anywhere else in Gloucestershire. You would not find such a problem in Painswick or Chipping Campden! Perhaps the county planners take the view that Cam does not matter. Come on Cam residents, action please! Stand up for your rights. Lobby your councillors.

Two views from the top of Cam Pitch in 1959 prior to the building of the Summerhayes Estate. How narrow the road seems in the top picture, with the houses in Fairmead visible on the right-hand side. The bottom picture show Cam Mills with Frocester Hill as a backdrop.

The Avenue leading to Stinchcombe in 1974, just two years before the devastation of Dutch elm disease.

Two views of High Street. The top picture is of 1960, the bottom picture, of 1968, shows the new fish and chip shop.

Cam Pitch in the snow, *c*. 1920. A turnpike bar originally stood in this road roughly where the gas lamp is.

Many of the cottages in Lower Cam were built in the 1820s by Reuben Hill, referred to on page 113. Hill invested £4,500 in purchasing land, a huge sum when the average weaver's weekly wage was just eight shillings. Cottages in Rowley and probably Chapel Street were part of this speculation. In the halcyon 1820s he built seventy cottages in Cam, mainly for weavers, each cottage capable of holding two handlooms. He received rentals of between £6 and £9 a year per cottage. The collapse of the woollen cloth industry in the 1830s devalued his investment by three-quarters, and many weavers left, no longer able to afford the tenancies. From this time the population declined, many people emigrating to America or the colonies. The local economy was devastated and little building took place in the village apart from a few red brick villas at the end of the century.

The junction of Chapel Street and High Street in 1957.

The Berkeley Arms, *c.* 1916.

The High Street, with Cam Meeting manse on the left-hand side, c. 1910. This house was the manse for about 160 years, until it became a shop in the 1920s.

This view of High Street was probably little changed from 1838 when William Augustus Miles reported on the distress among the weavers: 'There are about eighty weavers in this parish, nearly all of whom are employed, yet notwithstanding there was an appearance of poverty and destitution in their houses, in almost every one of which there was sickness of some kind among the children or the parents; several I counted with measles, others with whooping cough, and some wasting away from consumption.

'Although the weavers' houses are generally a scene of confusion and dirt, they appear to be quite unaware of the fact, thus verifying an old proverb, "Habit is second nature."

'I do not think it is the natural inclination of the weavers to live in a state so comfortless and cheerless; but in many cases it is the unavoidable consequence of large families and small cottages; thus you find them washing, drying, cooking, weaving, quilling (winding the thread on to a bobbin), and all the other necessary culinary and working duties performed in one small apartment, which is as prejudicial to health, from its atmospherical impurities, as it is destitute of comfort, cleanliness, and order.

'The poor people, generally speaking, live upon vegetables, chiefly cabbage and potatoes; and it is probable that an exclusive vegetable aliment has the tendency to produce those disorders on the bowels which are so prevalent among the poor weavers, not only in this, but in other parishes.'

Two views of High Street, the top picture *c.* 1900, the bottom picture *c.* 1920. Note the haystack in the top picture. The buildings shown in the bottom picture are those at the extreme right in the top view.

Thatched cottages in High Street, *c.* 1900. Many of the cottage properties built prior to 1800 were thatched rather than stone tiled or slated. Although only a little more than a mile from the stone quarries on the hills around Dursley, or Upper Cam with the stone quarries on Cam Long Down, the old cottages in Lower Cam tended to be built with locally quarried sandstone, or soft, poor quality limestone. The stone around Dursley, the inferior oolite, is suitable for rough ashlar stone blocks but not hard enough to cut stone slates. The clay pantiles came into common use around 1820, Welsh slate just twenty years later, but good old thatch still kept most of the rain out.

An unusual view looking over Lower Cam with Cam Peak as a backdrop.

This view came from a postcard made out of a real photograph, rather than the more usual collotype reproductions used for postcards. Because of the quality of the original it has been possible to enlarge the image as shown below. The old lady is wearing traditional costume. This photograph shows Yew Tree Villas and the Jubilee Tree planted in 1897 to commemorate the Diamond Jubilee of Queen Victoria. This would date this photograph to about 1901.

Middle Mills, *c.* 1905. So named for the obvious reason of falling between Cam Mill and Draycott Mill. The mill was originally a woollen mill, an iron foundry by 1816 and a grist mill for corn by 1823.

Draycott Mill, *c.* 1915 in the top photograph, *c.* 1905 below. Originally a woollen mill, Draycott converted to a grist mill at some time before 1801 and remained as such until modern times, when operated by Workman Brothers.

Another view of Draycott Mill, *c.* 1910, showing the width of the main road at this time.

A fine photograph of Coaley Junction, *c.* 1910, with a passenger train standing on the platform for Dursley. The staff pose for this photograph of the Midland Railway Company in its prime.

Coaley Junction in 1961 – the end of the line. Passenger services to Dursley were stopped in 1962 but the station remained open and trains on services to Gloucester and Bristol continued to stop here for several more years. Shortly after, this unusual 1850s station building was demolished. Now the trend is for re-opening such halts. How short-sighted the dramatic cuts of the 1960s now seem.

COALEY. 3632.

The Swan Inn, Coaley, *c.* 1930. The village of Coaley has not had a good press down the ages. In 1639 William Smith, steward of the Berkeley Estate, complained of the dirty streets, and Samuel Rudder, writing in 1779, went further: 'The public roads here are the worst that can be conceived; and the poor labouring people are so abandoned to nastiness, that they throw everything within a yard or two of their doors, where the filth makes a putrid stench, to the injury of their own health, and the annoyance of travellers, if any come among them.' On a happier note, Smith mentions jollities on Coaley Peak, just a few years before the Civil War: 'The most eminent hill is called Cowley Pike; where to behold young men and maids ascending and descending and boys tumbling down, especially on Communion days in the afternoons what times the resort is greatest, bringeth no small delight to many of the elder sort also delighting therein.'

The depression created by the collapse of the woollen industry was felt most injuriously in Coaley, where the parish had descended to squalor in the relative good times so that the bad times brought starvation and disaster. In 1838 the population was 1,124, but this was reduced by emigration, and now, one hundred and fifty years later, the population has begun to recover. There were 762 souls in 1971, rising to 837 in 1981. The 1991 census figures are not yet available.

The parish squalor is commented upon by William Miles in his report of 1839: 'Perhaps no parish has been so unfortunate as Coaley as regards its clergymen, or more neglected in every sense by those who ought at once to be the advisers and the pattern of the people. Of the three last clergymen, one committed suicide, and the other was a confirmed drunkard. In such a state of things it is no matter of surprise that the poor should be lax in their morals, degraded as to intellect, or rude and barbarous in their manners. At a coroner's inquest there was only one man out of the twelve jurymen who could write his name. Several of these men were handloom weavers. Nor does this state of ignorance confine itself to the lower classes, but it is, I am told, observable in the farmers or others: in fact, take the parish throughout, a worse in morals or intellect cannot be found.'

Celebrations in the Street. Probably the village's contribution to the Diamond Jubilee of 1897 or the coronation of Edward VII in 1902. The Victorian church school can be seen on the right-hand side of the picture. It was no thanks to the curate of Coaley in 1837 that this came to be built for, in a written reply to William Miles on the subject of education, he wrote a spleenful and vitriolic attack on education and the people of Coaley: 'As far as the branches of knowledge are concerned, which are essential towards rendering persons capable of superintending their own business and guarding their own interests, no additional means of education are required. The disposition of the working classes at Coaley is inimical to instruction generally; and it is only by adopting a system of patient, mild, and persevering exhortation, that they can be led at all to fall in with the views of their clergyman on that point.' He did not answer Miles's question on education at all, but his tirade equated learning with the learning of vice and debauchery arising from the numerous village beer shops. Perhaps his reactionary view was due in no small way to having one vicar who was a suicide and another who was himself a drunkard. 'So many haunts of vice and wickedness; schools where insipient vice is matured to crime, and infamy, and eternal ruin. Would to G they might be suppressed from one end of the land to the other . . . It must also be borne in mind that the poverty of the class whose interests are now sought to be promoted, arise in great measure from habits of personal intemperance; and although, doubtless, the introduction of machinery some years ago must have tended greatly to depress the honest and sober workman, yet it is a positive fact, that it matters not in most cases what extent of wages may be earned, the majority will, as opportunity allows, spend the greater portion in the licensed houses for drunkards and dissipated wretches.'

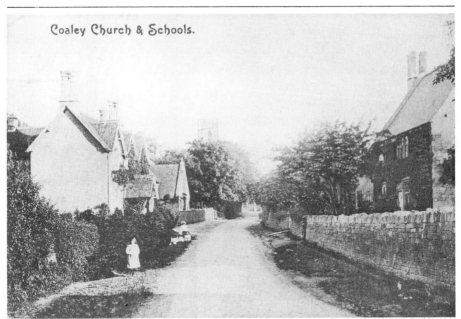

Two similar views of the Street, looking towards the church, *c.* 1904. The people look most respectable – universal education from the village school had obviously had far greater effect than our conservative curate would have considered possible.

A view at Far Green, *c.* 1902, with the chapel in the distance which has now been converted to a private dwelling.

Knapp Farm, *c.* 1930, with Coaley Wood on the right-hand side, taking us back to the top of Crawley Hill, the starting point of our peregrination. And with the words of our Anglican curate still ringing in our ears, we turn instead to the adage of Dr Johnson, and walk down Crawley for a quick one at the Top Crown. For after such a lengthy walk, it must surely be opening time.